Withdrawn

Aye-Aye

by Dawn Bluemel Oldfield

Consultant: Darin Collins, DVM
Director, Animal Health Programs
Woodland Park Zoo
Seattle, Washington

BEARPORT
PUBLISHING

New York, New York

Credits

Cover, © javarman3/iStock; TOC, © CSP_dennisvdwater/AGE Fotostock; 4–5, © Thorsten Negro/ image BROKER/Alamy; 6–7, © Frans Lanting/MINT Images/Science Source; 6, © Damian Ryszawy/Shutterstock; 8TL, © Nigel Cattlin/FLPA/Minden Pictures; 8TR, © Art_man/Shutterstock; 8B, © GlobalP/iStock; 9, © Konrad Wothe/NPL/Minden Pictures; 9R, © Onyx9/Shutterstock; 10L, © Eric Isselee/Shutterstock; 10–11, © Nick Garbutt/Nature Picture Library/Alamy; 12, © Lynn M. Stone/Nature Picture Library; 13, © Chris Hellier/Alamy; 14–15, © Nick Garbutt/NPL/Minden Pictures; 16T, © Wothe/blickwinkle/Alamy; 16B, © Nick Garbutt/Nature Picture Library/Alamy; 17, © Thorsten Negro/imageBROKER/Alamy; 18T, © Mark Carwardine/NPL/Minden Pictures; 18B, © Robert Pickett/Papilio /Alamy; 19, © Yuri Shibnev/Nature Picture Library; 20T, © Nick Garbutt/RGB Ventures/SuperStock/Alamy; 20B, © Nick Garbutt/NPL/Minden Pictures; 21, © Albert Visage/FLPA/Minden Pictures; 22 (T to B), © Enjoylife2/iStock, © Mitsuyoshi Tatematsu/Nature Production/Minden Pictures, and © Mitsuyoshi Tatematsu/Minden Pictures; 23TL, © Dimitios Vlassis/Shutterstock; 23TR, © Karel Gallas/Shutterstock; 23BL, © Ivan Kuzmin/ Shutterstock; 23BR, © Abeselom Zerit/Shutterstock.

Publisher: Kenn Goin
Senior Editor: Joyce Tavolacci
Creative Director: Spencer Brinker
Design: Debrah Kaiser
Photo Researcher: Thomas Persano

Library of Congress Cataloging-in-Publication Data
Names: Bluemel Oldfield, Dawn, author..
Title: Aye-aye / by Dawn Bluemel Oldfield.
Description: New York, New York : Bearport Publishing, 2018. | Series: Even
    weirder and cuter | Includes bibliographical references and index.
Identifiers: LCCN 2017039211 (print) | LCCN 2017046419 (ebook) |
ISBN 9781684025268 (ebook) | ISBN 9781684024681 (library)
Subjects: LCSH: Aye-aye—Juvenile literature.
Classification: LCC QL737.P935 (ebook) | LCC QL737.P935 B58 2018 (print) |
    DDC 599.8/3—dc23
LC record available at https://lccn.loc.gov/2017039211

For more information, write to Bearport Publishing Company, Inc., 45 West 21st Street, Suite 3B, New York, New York 10010. Printed in the United States of America.

10 9 8 7 6 5 4 3 2 1

Contents

What's this weird but cute animal?

LARGE ears!

It's an aye-aye (EYE-eye).

Yellow
eyes!

Long
fingers!

5

Where in the world do these odd animals live?

Aye-ayes are found only in Madagascar.

They live in thick forests.

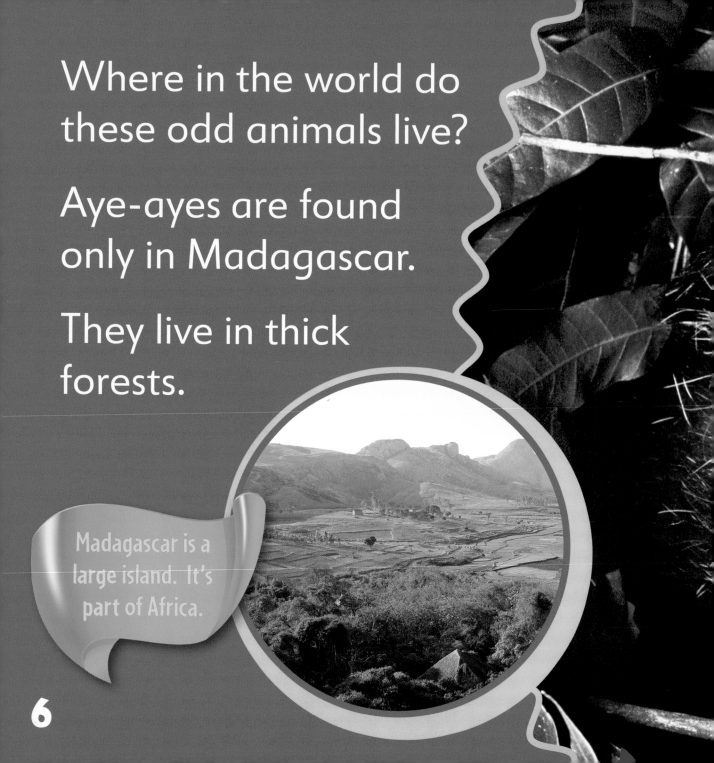

Madagascar is a large island. It's part of Africa.

An aye-aye has long teeth like a rat and big ears like a bat.

It also has a bushy tail like a fox.

Yet, it's a kind of lemur.

8

A lemur is a monkey-like animal. Lemurs, along with gorillas and humans, are **primates**.

How big is an aye-aye?

It's about the size of a pet cat.

An aye-aye weighs about 5 pounds (2 kg)—or as much as a bag of sugar.

tail

The animal's bushy tail is as long as its body.

Look at those fingers and toes!

An aye-aye has a long and super skinny finger on each hand.

The finger looks like a twig!

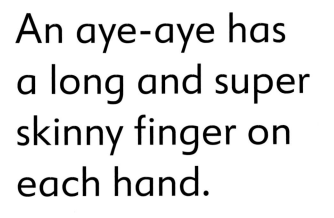

claw

Aye-ayes have sharp claws.

long, skinny middle finger

13

Good night!

Aye-ayes are **nocturnal**.

Their big yellow eyes help them see in the dark.

An aye-aye has great hearing, too. It can move its ears toward a sound without moving its head!

14

An aye-aye leaps through the moonlit sky.

It jumps from tree to tree.

The creature is looking for something to eat.

Aye-ayes have a nickname—the "king of treetops."

What's for dinner?

Aye-ayes eat fruit, seeds, and **grubs**.

fruit

coconut

Aye-ayes travel up to 3 miles (5 km) each night to find food.

18

Grubs often live deep inside trees.

grub

How does an aye-aye locate a grub?

19

Tap, tap, tap!

The aye-aye taps on the tree and listens for grubs.

When it finds one, it **gnaws** a hole in the bark.

20

Finally, the aye-aye stabs the juicy grub with its thin middle finger!

grub

Aye-ayes' large front teeth never stop growing.

21

More Odd Primates

Golden Lion Tamarin
The golden lion tamarin is a small primate that lives in Brazil. It has a golden mane like a lion!

Gray Mouse Lemur
The gray mouse lemur is the world's smallest primate! Its tail is twice as long as its body. It weighs about as much as ten pennies.

Pygmy Marmoset
The pygmy marmoset lives in rain forests in South America. This tiny primate can rest on a person's finger!

Glossary

gnaws (NAWZ) keeps biting or nibbling on something

grubs (GRUHBZ) the wormlike larvae of some insects

nocturnal (nok-TUR-nuhl) active at night

primates (PRYE-mayts) animals that include lemurs, monkeys, gorillas, and humans

Index

Read More

Owings, Lisa. *Aye-Aye (Extremely Weird Animals).* Minnetonka, MN: Bellwether (2014).

Rake, Jody Sullivan. *The Aye-Aye (Weird Animals).* Mankato, MN: Capstone (2008).

Learn More Online

To learn more about aye-ayes, visit **www.bearportpublishing.com/EvenWeirderAndCuter**

About the Author

Dawn Bluemel Oldfield is a writer. She enjoys reading, traveling, and gardening. She and her husband live in Texas.